A SHIBUMI ENTERPRISE PUBLICATION PO BOX 8780 PITTSBURGH PA, 15221

BLOCK2LAPTOP@GMAIL.COM SHIBUMIENT.COM

From the Block to the Laptop An Ex-Offenders Guide to Online Success

ISBN: 9781092656979 Imprint: Independently published EBook

ISBN: 9781092656979 Imprint: Independently published

# Dedication

My biggest thanks goes to **my Mother and Sister**.Thank you for supporting me in all the things that I've been threw in life.

A second thanks goes out to my good friend James L. Hairston, author of Federal Nightmare ft. Drive-By for encouraging me to put things in motion.

My third thanks goes to Cyber Service for helping me do a lot of research for this book.

And most of all, thanks to all the readers for putting your trust in me and buying my book. I hope that you will be able to create massive income with the ideas and tactics in this book.

I would also like to thank myself for learning how to create income from hard work, making mistakes and learning from them...

# FROM THE BLOCK TO THE LAPTOP

<u>An ex-offenders guide to online success</u>

By
Gerald W. Eiland

# Table of Contents

# FROM THE BLOCK TO THE LAPTOP

So far so good, you've made it out of prison. What now? For better or the worst, it's all up to you.

Your family and friends will try to help you as much as they can to get back on your feet and help you find a good paying job. Then you find out that good paying jobs are few and far between for a felon that has the parole board attached at the hip. Having a $10 an hour wage job, your whole paycheck is going towards paying bills. You barely have enough money to buy a decent meal. But, without a job your future will be uncertain. You'll be in danger of repeating crimes that landed you in prison in the first place.

There are not a lot of businesses out there that is willing to take a chance on an ex-offender without starting from the bottom at the lowest paying position available. This is the reason why I am writing this book. So as to help you identify the skills you need to become successful.

I know some of you may be a little optimistic about starting a business after spending a large amount of time in prison. Optimism is a characteristic of many ex-offenders. Optimism can be the fuel that propels you through obstacles that would stop the average person in their tracks.

Some ex-offenders have thought about reverting to their old habits wondering why they cannot seem to get ahead. It is because some people are just looking for a hand out and do not have any ambition. Some will be content with a minimum wage job living from paycheck to paycheck. Getting welfare on the side.

If you are reading this book. It means that you have the ability to think positively and never let your brain delude your ability to become successful against all odds, which will be your greatest asset. Spending time in prison is hard to prepare for a successful reentry, but you've managed to survive through, crazy and often time dangerous maze. Now that you're older and hopefully wiser, you have the opportunity to completely turn your life around.

You'll soon discover that with a criminal background few employers will want to hire you. With the widespread use of criminal background checks, your employer can find out everything that you ever been locked up for. In fact nowadays, you can just Google someone to find out everything about him or her.

There's no sense in lying on your job application because there is no place to hide these days. Unfortunately, some ex-offenders become re-offenders. In fact correctional institutions do very minimum to insure that ex-offenders don't become re-offenders. The system works against your best interest with a criminal record, you'll face challenges that other people take for granted, like clothing, housing, transportation, internet access. You know the basic resources you need to survive and find a job upon your release. Many of you are only able to obtain low-paying jobs. Jobs that require no thought. These jobs will be manual labor positions such as construction laborers, warehouse workers, car washers and food preparers. You know the real crappy jobs that no one else wants to do. These positions are what you call 'Dead end jobs'. You know the kind that if you work hard you'll be promoted to burgers and fries. However, I guess it is at least a starting point. You have to start from somewhere to get on your feet just make sure you never become content in these positions. Use these positions as a stepping-stone to move on to bigger and better things. I know that a lot of you have read some sort of booklet or pamphlet informing you about different ex-offenders programs that is available to you upon your release. If you are fortunate enough to be able to partake in any of these programs. You should take advantage of them, take whatever type of computer classes that's available. Such as computer literacy and typing, these classes will be vital to becoming successful online. Knowledge is the key to success.

In this book, you will learn everything from internet marketing strategies outsourcing tips and how to utilize certain websites to your advantage I will also help you to identify certain niches to help you get started.

I will be breaking down all aspects of how to make money and succeed online in an easy to understand terms.

It is my goal to give you all the tools and information you need to start making money online. It will be time consuming but the payoff will be great. I started with no experience, no training. With no support, I figured it all out on my own and ultimately started to make a lot of money online and so will you.

No matter what type of online business you want to start, this guide can really help you, you'll be able to work from anywhere in the world from your laptop with an internet connection.

Here are some internet terminology explained

Internet marketing

It is the marketing of a product or service over the internet. Internet marketing may also be referred as e-marking, web marketing, and online marketing. So if you promote your business, product, service, or website online its internet marketing. It is very popular because the set up cost is minimal and you can reach customers and clients worldwide.

In order to make money online, you should have some basic knowledge of internet marketing. Through this book, I will share with you some of the knowledge I've gained over time, I will show you some very helpful websites, tips, and tools to help you get started. I will explain the exact steps to take when setting up a new website. People create websites for one or two reasons and that is to inform or to generate income.

I will be explaining many different ways to generate income online. This book will give you an overview of money making possibilities on the internet. You must find the one that works best for you. You will have to study and analyze and research whatever niche you choose and stick with it until you have mastered it.

A niche is the type of product or service you will sell. You could be in a niche that sells clothing or a sub-niche that sells jeans. A sub niche is a market within a market. The internet is ideal for finding niches. Your niche doesn't have to be something that you are personally interested in. Your motivation should be the money aspect of it. If you don't already have a niche that you are interested in. You would have to do some research to find one.

Once you do your research and have made a list of ideas for your niche, you would have to analyze those things to see if it's a profitable niche. I will go into more details about how to research your niche later on in this book.

Affiliate marketing

It is when a person drives visitors to a person's web site or place of business and gets paid commission when the customer buys something by clicking on the link that is on the affiliate's website. The affiliate brings traffic to a merchant's place of business and gets paid commission only when a sale is made. E-books is an electronic book, which is also known as a digital book. It's called a digital product because you're able to download it immediately after you've purchased it. It's basically a regular book in electronic format.

You're able to read it from your computer or from another device such as e-book readers like the amazon's kindle. An e-book is usually delivered in pdf format to the buyer. You can buy an e-book any time of the day from a website on the internet using your credit card or PayPal account and you will be reading your new e-book in under five minutes, clickbank.com is a digital marketplace for more than 100,000 digital products and vendors. They process more than 30,000 digital transactions a day. Clickbank.com is also the largest affiliate marketplace on the internet. They mostly sell digital products: e-books, software, and videos. They sell a wide range of how to digital products and just about everything else that you can think of. Because all of these products are digital there is no shipping cost. The commission rates for affiliates are very high, between %50 to %70 or more.

Clickbank is where you can find affiliates to sell your products. If you have created a digital product, you can become a vender on clickbank and put your product on there for anybody to sell.

## Article marketing

This is when you write an article with keywords, which will make it easier for your article to rank in search engines such as Google. When a person read your article with your keywords in it, you would then send that person to your website to be a prospect in what product or services that your website is providing.

## Opt-in box

An opt-in box is somewhere for your visitor to enter their email address to receive emails from you. Once a visitor gives you their email address, they have opt-in. Opt-in means when someone is given the option to receive bulk emails from you that is sent to a lot of people that have opt-in to receive information of some kind such as, a newsletter or advertising which is called a mailing list.

You should obtain permission before sending emails because without it your email is considered unsolicited bulk email, also known as spam. When someone opt-in to your mailing list you should confirm it by a double opt-in. By this when a new subscriber is asked to subscribe to your mailing list, you would send them a confirmation email telling them that they will begin to receive emails from you. The new subscriber must respond to the confirmation email before they will be added to the mailing list.

## Email marketing

This is one of the most effective ways to keep customers coming back and to market your products or services directly to their inbox. All you have to do is send to people that have opted-in, then email them on a regular basis with links that will earn you money. You would have to sell yourself first. People don't like to just keep receiving email asking them to buy products. You would have to offer something of value for free every now and then. People like to receive free stuff they could use, it could be free information or some sort of digital product. This will give you a better chance of selling to them on a regular basis, it's like lead generation. You make a sell on the backend.

## Autoresponder

This is a program that automatically sends out emails on a predetermined basis to all the opt-in people on your mailing list. Once you have built a mailing list, this is when you send them free information such as newsletter or an affiliate link. You could also market your offers to the people on your list. It would be too time consuming to do all of this manually each time you receive a new opt-in. An autoresponder does all this for you automatically. If you want to send out multiple email, you could set the intervals for the emails for like twice a day. All you have to do is type in the email once in your autoresponder software, your list will get an email twice a day, and anyone who joins your list will automatically be sent those emails for the next five days. An owner of a list uses an autoresponder software to send out a sequence of emails that goes out at regular intervals. It's a must that you have an auto responder when you have an opt-in box on your web site. http://aweber.com is one of the best auto responders that is getting traffic to your website. It means getting people to see your website and getting them to buy your product or service. There are many different techniques you can use to get people to see your site such as social media, blogs, and pay-per-click. Affiliates conversion rate is how many people that sees your ad and make a purchase from your site. If your ad is shown 100 times a realistic conversion rate would be anywhere between 1% to 10% anything above this in the internet marketing business is considered excellent If you can increase your conversion rate, you'll increase your profits without worrying about getting more traffic.

## SEO

This stands for Search Engine Optimization. It's the process of ranking your website in Google. In the natural listings by following certain keyword related rules when using SEO technique, if applied correctly it can result in the search engine ranking your site on the first page so that your website can be easily found using certain keywords.

## Blog

A blog is something like a website, which is updated regularly by the owner. When updating a blog it's called blogging and that person whom manages the blog, is called a blogger. The blogger puts regular updated content, which is called blog posts, which are written on a particular niche, where people can share ideas and learn from other peoples comments and they are also able to do business with other people in the same niche.

## Landing page

This is where you start off by building your list, to convert visitors into customers this is where you get prospects to fill in their personal information, such as email address and first name the landing page is mostly used for marketing. A lot of pay-per-click campaigns will send you to a landing page. Sometimes, a website with an opt-in box which is usually called a squeeze page.

## Sales page

This is nothing more than a one page sales letter with a "buy it now" button on it. These sales pages are so professional written that it makes people think that they really need to buy this product. They are written in such a persuasive way they influence visitors to buy the product. A good converting sales page is an art that is done by a professional.

## Pay-per-click

This is one of the best ways to get traffic to your site. Payperclick is an advertising method used on search engines, advertising networks, blogs, and content based websites. The advertiser, which is you will only pay when a user clicks on its ad with pay per click advertising caption. Your website can be seen by thousands of people when a prospect types in a keyword matching your keyword, the search engine will show your ad. The traffic that you will receive will be targeted. All you'll have to do is set up an ad campaign with the keywords that you want to use in order to use as pay-per-click campaign. You would have to sign up for an account with some network and write an advertisement, then make a landing page for your ads this could be your own website or an affiliate link you would also have to make a keyword list or ad campaign. Then set up how much you would want to bid for those keywords on a pay-per-click network. When someone clicks on an ad, the advertiser has to pay Google money, this is what is called pay per click. The advertiser only has to pay when the visitor clicks on the website.

## AdSense

This is when a website owner wants Google to place a relevant ad on its website. Each time someone clicks on the ad, Google pays the website owner on the per click basis.

## Niche

You have to find a niche before you can start making money online. This could be something that you are passionate about or it could just be something that you think you can make a lot of money on. It's not unusual to find a niche that you know nothing about, your motivation should be the money aspect of it. I'm about to disclose numerous sites and suggestions that can help you find a new niche. Always keep in mind when researching your niche, why do people spend money, most people spend money online to solve a problem they are having or to fill a basic need or for their entertainment. Here's how to use Amazon to find a new niche. http:// www.amazon.com/gp/bestseller Amazon is a great place to find a new niche . Amazon is also a trending site, if you want to know the best-selling item on amazon, you would just go to the site above to see what the best-selling product is in whatever category you choose. Just type in any keyword and you would be presented with sub categories on the left side of the page, just browse and get some ideas when doing research on amazon, you can search under different methods like:

Customer reviews, new, popular, publication, date, price, relevance, check out screen shot, you could also search by department. This will give you 100 of categories and 1,000 of sub categories to check out. You could also check out Amazon hot new release section at http://www.amazon.com/gp/new-releases/.

Here are some auction sites to find a niche.
 www.flippa.com
 www.ebay.com
 www.ebay.com/cln


Here you can check out the trending collections on www.popular.ebay.com. Here you can find out what's popular on www.ebay.com/ctg.


Here are some informational sites to find niches www.freeindex.com.

Here you can search the selections of categories of businesses and events to find a new niche on www.alltop.com , this is a blog site and it's all about
niches.

www.answers.yahoo.com/dir/index is a great site for niches, were people tell you what their problems are.

[www.answerbag.com](www.answerbag.com) this site is where people are asking questions on a topic, it's also a great place to find content for you r product .

[www.theanswerbank.com](www.theanswerbank.com) on this site you can read some of the questions and answers to find a new niche, they have different categories.

[www.ask.com](www.ask.com) on this site they have multiple selections like "popular questions", how to questions" and "what is questions" the how to questions are people that are looking for a solution to a problem.

**Clickbank** ([www.clickbank.com)](www.clickbank.com) if you are determine to make money online then clickbank is a great place to start. Clickbank is the largest digital information broker in the world. If you have a niche for an eBook or any other digital product then clickbank is the place to start.

**Clickbank analytics:** on this site you can find information on any of the products listed on clickbank , just browse the categories to find a new niche.

Here are some clickbank analytics websites:

[www.cb-analytics.com](www.cb-analytics.com)
[www.clickbankanalytics.net](www.clickbankanalytics.net)
[www.cnengine.com](www.cnengine.com)
[www.cbtrends.com](www.cbtrends.com)
[www.cbgraph.com](www.cbgraph.com)

**Google** is another good place to find new niches.

**Google apps:** Type in a keyword in Google and choose "apps" from the drop down menu under more and Google will show you a list of apps if there's an app o n the market .

**Google images:** Search for any keywords and click "images" and Google will tell you what people are looking for related to your image.

Google how to: If you type in "how to" into Google. Google will automatically tell you what people are searching for and how to find a solution to a problem.

**Google news:** You can type in any keyword and click on the drag menu under "more" then select news. Google will give you the latest news on your keyword, a great place to find a new niche.

**Google video:** Type in any keyword into Google and click video you can browse to get new ideas for a new niche.

Google blogs: http://google.com/?tbm=blg. On this site it will bring up a screen where you can see "search blogs" just type in your keyword and Google will bring up blogs related to your keyword.

**Google discussions:** Go to https://google.com//tbm=dsc. This will bring up a screen where you will see "search discussion" just type in your keyword and Google will bring up discussions related to your keyword.

**Google scholar:** Type in your keyword in www.scholar.google.com and you will get a lot of information to find niches and sub-niches,

Google alert: If you have found your niche, you can find out more about it by using Google alert. Using Google alert you will be informed by email every time someone talks about blogs or say anything about your niche or keyword. You will get emails at intervals each time someone mentions your niche. When Google alerts you on blogs that is talking about your niche you need to write them down and visit them. You can email the blog or website that you received in your inbox from Google alert saying that you have a product or book that they can put on their website, this is a good method to find affiliates to sell your product.

**Google zeitgeist:** To find out what people have been searching for, they publish a report every year on the top stories, trends, and topics that were most popular over the year and is available in over 70 countries.

**Google hot trends:** www.google.com/trends/hottrends here you can find the most search for topic of the day also check out www.google.com/trends/topcharts?zg=full

**Google correlate:** Go to www.google.com/trends/correlate Type in any keyword then hit "search correlate "and it will give you other suggestions that follow the same trend as your keyword.

Google top 10: Here you can search [top 10], [top 50] and [top 100] of something. For example: [top 10 best workouts], [ top 10 best hosting] etc. Then just click on the website in your search and find your new niche.

Google list of: Search in google for [list of something] e.g. [list of diets] [list of dogs] etc. Just browse to find a new niche.

### Use wiki to find a new niche
**Wikianswers**: www.wiki.answers.com you will find their categories on the home page, browse to find niche, you could also look at their content page here; http://www.answers.com/main/what/content they also have a video answering section too. http://videoanswers.com Find the newer questions here http://wiki.answers.com/q/newq

**Answers:** www.answers.com they have over 4 million topics on this site

**Wikihow categories:** www.wikihow.com This site is on information on how to do things, they have a collection of quality guides to learn a new skill to find ideas for a new niche. Click explore on the home page then click on categories.

**Wikipedia:** www.wikipedia.org Here you can find information on just about any topic you can think of. You can find a list of the main categories here: http://en.wikipedia.org/wiki/portal:content/categories here is a list of more wiki's to explore

**Wiktionary:** http://www.wiktionary.com
**Wikidata:** http://wikidata.org/wiki/wikidata:mainpage
**Wikivoyage:** https://www.wikivoyage.org
**Wikinews:** https://www.wikinews.org/
**Wikiquote:** https://www.wikiquote.org
**Wikisource:** https://wikisource.org/wiki/mainpage
**Wikibooks:** https://www.wikibooks.org
**Mediawiki:** https://www.mediawiki.org/wiki/mediawiki
**Wikiversity:** https://www.wikiversity.org
**Meta-wiki:** https://meta.wikimedia.org/wiki/mainpage

Online money making ideas website needed in this section of the book. I'll go over some methods you can use to make money from home, you will need your own website. Building a Website is not hard nor is it expensive I will go into more details on how to build your website later on in this book.

## Make Money

Make money from your website and blog. www.wordpress.com, this website can allow you to start your own blog for free, it is very simple, no programming skills needed. After you have set up your blog in your niche you can start publishing content on the Wordpress dashboard (a very friendly blogger interface) your purpose should be to get as many readers as you can. It should be interesting content that will capture people's attention and they would want to share with others and comment on. This can be done by choosing a popular niche you can promote your own product or services, or an affiliate's product with an affiliate link so that you would be paid a commission for sending your affiliate the sale, more on affiliates later, this is how you make your blogging produce revenue.

When you write about a popular niche or topic, your content will automatically be indexed by Google. People will be able to find your blog by typing in your keywords via search results when good SEO is applied. Never rely on one source of traffic you can use other methods to promote your blog. The most commonly used method is by commenting on other peoples blogs that are in the same niche as yours. By using this method, people will be motivated to check your blog out just out of curiosity. Once you have a high volume of traffic you can start putting AdSense and affiliate links on your blog to make a killing and a lot of affiliates on Clickbank will want to sell your ebook on that niche. You could also create your own eBook or some other product relating to your niche and sell it or give it away for free to get people to sign up to your opt-in box this way you will be building your mailing list which can make you tons of money on demand just by sending out emails to your subscribers.You will also have to send out free content to your subscribers, it could be a short report on your niche, a video, an e-book or anything of value to persuade people to input their email address.

## HERE IS A SAMPLE OF WHAT AN OPT-IN BOX LOOKS LIKE

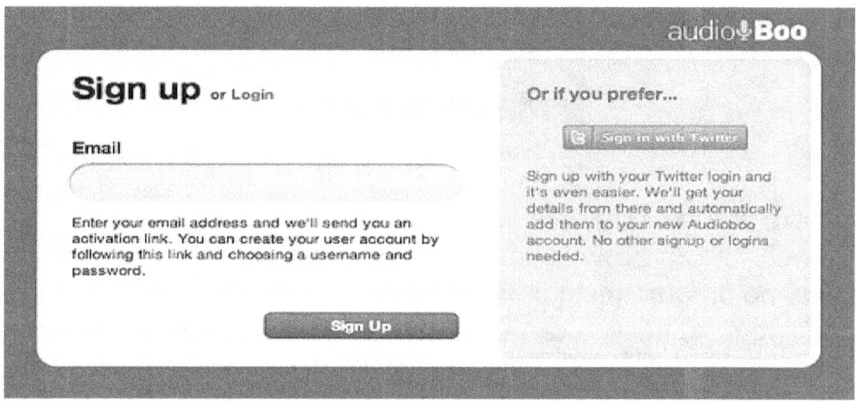

You can use www.worldinternetoffice.com to create an opt-in form.

## Auto blogging

You can set up a Wordpress blog that updates itself with the program like word press robot, you can set up a blog and never touch it again. All you have to do is input a few keywords that will describe your niche and then it will go and find content all over the internet and post it on your blog, and it's that simple.

You can program on how often you want it to post, where you want it to get content from like wiki articles sites, Wikipedia, and Google news and so on.

What kinds of ads you want to be displayed like amazon, AdSense and so on, how you want the content to be arranged. You can literally just program your blog and just forget about it while it grows and earn you money. You can find out more about wordpress robot at http://wprobot.det/ the down side to this is that your content will not be unique especially if other blogger has the same niche as yours and have auto blogging on their blog. Create a digital product and market it. If you have a certain subject that you are passionate about then you can write an eBook on it. This will be something of value that you can sell online if you have done your research on your new niche and find out that there is no e-book on it. This could mean only one or two things: either there is not a demand for such book or that yours will be the only one and you will make a killing and a lot of affiliates on Clickbank will want to sell your eBook. Make sure you do your due diligence to see if your keywords has produced a lot of searches. If your keywords in your niche has produced a lot of searches each month then it might be a good idea to write an eBook on that niche. In order to sell your eBook you will need a website and a download page so that your customer will be able to download their e-book after they have purchased it and if you want affiliates to sell your eBook then you will need to create an affiliate page as well if you decide to create an eBook you will need to create a sales page that will persuade people to purchase your eBook with the high conversion numbers of very well written sales pages you will generate a lot of income, you will also be able to increase your mailing list. One page sales page really works, just go to www.clickbank.com and you will be able to see that it is full of one page sales page. Clickbank is the biggest marketer for digital products and makes a sale every three seconds. Therefore, that lets you know that they work.

If you want help writing a sales copy for your eBook or any of the writing on your website you could outsource it to anyone of these sites.

www.elance.com
www.fiverr.com
www.freelancer.com
www.mocroworkers.com
www.odeskresource.com
www.peopleperhour.com

The competitors always check to see what their competitors are doing and for the price of their eBooks Just search for "your keywords " on these sites.

www.abebooks.com
www.ebooks.com
www.bn.com

You should also try searching amazon's kindle books, you will also need to get the cover of your eBook created. To make no mistake about it, cover sales book, you can have it done professionally at one of these websites.

www.absolutecovers.com
www.coverfactory.com
www.designgururyan.com
www.20dollarbanners.com
www.ebookcovercreater.com
www.killercovers.com
www.logocreator.com

Here are recommended free websites that you can drive traffic to www.homewebsitcenter.com. On this site you can have a website with an e-book that you can sell, all you have to do is fill in your PayPal address and your website is ready. They have several niches to choose from, all you have to do is just drive traffic to your site and start making money. It's a great start for beginners to set their skills to driving traffic to their website. They also have a paid version that gives you a bunch of websites statistics. You can also check out www.weebly.com.

Some free websites make money by building a mailing list, this is a great method, but it will involve giving away a bunch of free stuff in exchange for getting an email address for future marketing, this method is so popular because your income will be limitless, just think if you have a 20,000 or more people on your mailing list you could make money on demand when you send out an email with your offer it's very easy to do just make sure the content that you give away is useful and relevant to your mailing list niche. Here are the things you need to get started:

- a domain name
- a website
- a squeeze page
- an autoresponder
- follow up emails

Your squeeze page is basically a headline with an opt-in box, the opt-in box is where people will input their email address and it will save it in your email list so that you will be able to send out email to your list of subscribers. You will have to send out free content to your subscribers. It could be a short report on your niche, a video, an e-book or anything of value to persuade people to input their email address.

## Opt-in Box

When people input their email address, they will automatically be added to your list and will receive free content in their inbox. The software that creates your opt-in forms will hold your list and send out emails automatically to your subscribers. The most popular auto responder is www. aweber.com.

Here are some more autoresponder s that you can check out:
www.1shoppingcart.com
www.mailchimp.com
www.listwire.com
www.constantcontact.com
www.infusionsoft.com

You can also buy pre-made landing squeeze page templates at a very reasonable price at these websites here:
www.buylandingpagedesign.com
www.landingpagemonkey.com
www.instapage.com
www.semanticlp.com
www.leadpages.com

When you set that up it's time to create pre written email to be automatically delivered to your mailing list these email should be designed to engage your subscribers and deliver valuable content.

The whole thing is to have your opt-in box automated so the only thing you would have to do is get traffic to your site and the system will take care of the rest by sending out free content and product offers.

Getting people on your mailing should be a piece of cake since you'll be giving away some free content that they are interested in, you could also get people on your mailing list by using solo ads, solo ads are email that you can send out to other peoples mailing list to promote your own list. This will not be for free of course you can make an offer to pay the person in the same niche as you, that has a list to send out promotional email with a link to your squeeze page. There subscribers would then visit your squeeze page and hopefully opt-in to your list.

List building is a great way to make money because it allows you to generate recurring income over and over again once you have set everything up properly.

By having an eye catching headline on your squeeze page that tell people the benefit of opting in and why they need the information that you are providing over the next few months can help you increase your list and you'll be able to promote your own products or CPA offers Affiliate links and so on to your list of subscribers and earn money, sell advertising space to earn money when you have generated a large mailing list. You can start earning money by selling advertising space on your website when using this method of conversion rate is important if not more important than traffic, it's important to put only ads that is related to your niche to succeed because you will be able to deliver ads to people that are likely to buy from the advertiser. So provide advertising to a targeted market.

You can contact website owners to ask them if they would like to place a banner, ad on your niche based website if you don't know how to design a banner ad you can outsource it to sites like www.elance.com you can also use www.20dollarbanners.com and have one made. The only thing you would need is a picture. In addition, when a prospect clicks on the picture they will automatically go to the advertiser's website, make sure that the advertiser's website opens up in a new browser window so your websites stays open. Make money with CPA (Cost Per Action), you can use this search engine to place ads and send them directly to your landing page with a CPA offer. This method is costly. However, once you've found a niche that works you can make a lot of money.

www.search.yahoo.com

www.bing.com

www.hotbot.com

www.lycos.com

www.searchenginenginecolossus.com is an international directory of search engines, buy and sell unclaimed luggage. Thousands of luggage gets lost every day around the world. These unclaimed luggage is usually sold at auctions in the united states. The unclaimed baggage center in Alabama receives 800,000 visitors a day. Below are some auctions sites that you can use to start the process of attending auctions for lost luggage. You never know what you might get out of these suitcases but it sounds like a lot of fun.

www.wellersauctions.com

www.unclaimedbaggage.com

www.hertsauctions.com

You can then sell these items in the luggage on sites like eBay or other auctions sites.

New product launches websites when a new product is being launched. You can start a website relating to it using keywords around the product and describe the pros and cons of the product, with your affiliate link all over the pages, make money with apps, you can create your own for iPhone, it's not that complicated here. It is a site where you can make an app for free

www.seaattleclouds.com

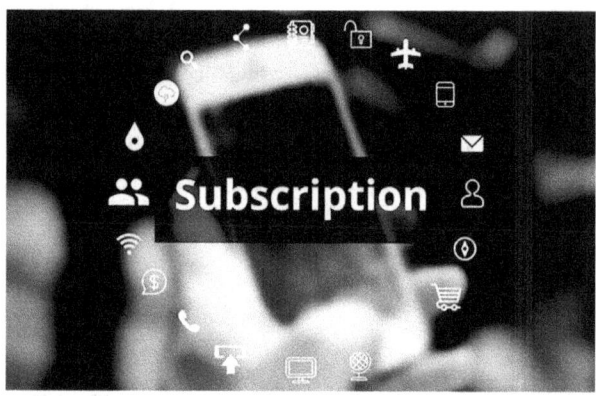

## Make money with a membership site

A membership site is a site that require a cost for people to receive informative information on your site. You would have to make it interesting. To sign up, you could charge a $1 to sign up for a one-week trial after a week of the $1 trial, their credit card will automatically charge them for the first month fee, unless they have asked for a refund this is why you must capture the customers interest with relevant content to keep them wanting more. You must spoon-feed them with interesting information every week to keep them signed up to your membership site, this means that every week you can deliver new content to your site, if they see all the content at the same.

Time is not an incentive for them to stay and they will want a refund after the first week. If they know that they will get fresh informative content every week they are more likely to stick around.

You can search for membership sites with keywords to see if there are any membership sites in your niche, if there is a high demand for your niche then a membership site is a great place to go before you start, you must have some informative information to tell your members each week and

month.

Membership sites charge anywhere between $7.99 to $19.99 you must make the sign up process simple and easy, if the process is long people will leave in the middle of the process.

Content is essential if you want to keep your members on your site. You must give your members their money's worth, the more fresh content you give them the more they would want to stick around. People love video content, to explain your content PLR videos are available online in a lot of different niches just Google " PLR video" and your "keyword".

Here are some sites with information on membership sites:

www.5minutemembershipsites.com
www.membershipsiteowner.com
www.membershipacademy.com

Here are some sites you can evaluate to get started:

www.yourmembership.com
www.amember.com
www.memberfire.com
www.easymemberpro.com also check out clickbank .com and look at the sites with high interest and that are selling well, analyze to gain more informative information for your niche.

## Make money from Dropshipping

Dropshipping is basically a supply chain management technique in which the seller (which is you) does not keep the goods in stock but transfers the customers' orders to a wholesaler or manufacturer who then ship the goods directly to the customer after the retailer pays for the purchase. The wholesaler or manufacturer ships the goods to the customer with the retailers name and address on the package as the sender, the retailer makes a profit on the difference between the wholesale and the retail price, it's a method of selling a product where the retailer will advertise the merchandise on his website and then the retailer will collect the money and then contact the wholesaler or manufacturer where the item is actually stored and have them ship the merchandise to the customer for a percentage of the profit. The consumer does not know that the wholesaler or manufacturer is involved in the process, this is a great way to make money online.

The thing about dropshipping is that you never have to worry about having inventory in a warehouse, the product stays in the warehouse until you have made an order and it will be shipped directly to your customer. All you have to do is to set up an account with a dropshipping supplier and get a list of their products and place them on your website.

Once someone order something from your website, you just forward the information to your supplier for fulfillment, you pay for the product and the supplier ships it directly to your customer.

Dropshipping can be a very profitable business. Once you have your website set up with merchandise from a reliable supplier and a PayPal account or credit card processing company all you need to do is drive traffic to your site.

You should choose products with a nice profit margin, the profit margin is what will be left over after expenses have been paid in full. After you have done your research you should be able to find products with a nice profit margin.

You must keep in mind that your customers don't know that the product they have just bought from you is being shipped from a dropshipper. Therefore, you must have customer service in case there is a problem, remember you are your customers direct contact. They will want to reach out if there is a problem for that reason, it's important to work with dropshippers that can solve problems in a reasonable amount of time and have good customer service. Types of dropshipping, the first is where you can search the web to do some niche research and find top selling niche products to sell then create your own website, you will also have to do more research to find a dropshipper for that product and set up an account with them, you will also have to learn about payment processors (merchant accounts) and shopping cart services for a small fee, you will be able to get started with a website with access to products that is pro loaded onto a readymade website for you, all you would have to do is drive traffic to your site to sell those products. It's a good idea to have multiple suppliers that stock the same product, so if one drop shipper don't have the product in stock then you will be able to use the other drop shipper, here is a list of popular drop shipping products to consider:

- Adult products-sex toys
- Baby products
- Body building products, e.g. Supplements, Protein shakes
- Camping gear
- Computer accessories
- Fishing gear
- Fitness products .

- Gardening items
- Gift baskets
- Gourmet coffee
- Hair accessories
- Hats
- Hunting gear
- Jewelry
- Laptop bags
- Luxury bedding
- Make up
- Massage products
- Maternity clothing
- Moccasins
- Motorcycle accessories
- Nanny cameras
- Plus size clothing
- Security cameras
- Solar items
- Spa items
- Big and tall clothing
- Toys
- T-shirts
- Vitamins and Supplements

Here are some dropshipping sites that you can check out, whichever dropshipping company you decide to work with, make sure you work with one that is certified. The certified dropshippers will give you photos that you can use on your website. They will also give you real wholesale prices and they won't charge you monthly fees or set up fees.

## Worldwide brands

www.worldwidebrands.com have wholesale products to sell online, they are one of the largest dropshippers out there, they add new suppliers weekly and have lots of training videos, they also have an exclusive members only forum.

www.doba.com this drop shipping company offers a variety of products, over a million to be exact. They are recommended by shopify most of the data is updated in real time, doba is a dropshipping agent who acts as a go between, between you and the wholesaler, doba passes your order directly to the wholesaler, that will deliver the product to the customer.

You can also find a product on doba and then try to find a supplier yourself, as the price will be cheaper.

Technically doba is not a drop shipper it's a service that connects, that helps connects retailers and wholesale suppliers together with an easier process than trying to do it on your own.

www.inventorysource.com This company has over half a million products in their database. With this company you won't have to pay any extra fees because you work directly with the wholesaler, the downside is that they don't offer a warranty or a return policy therefore if the product is damaged upon arrival or if the customer wants to return the product, you will have to deal with this problem on your own. Inventory source charges a monthly fee that range from $25 per month.

You can still have access to inventory source free but you won't be able to place any orders, they have several packages to choose from, some including readymade websites.

## Salehoo

www.salehoo.com they have a rather large number of suppliers with great wholesale prices, they have over a million products and over 8,000 suppliers, they have a little bit of everything, if you can't find your niche product here, give them a call and they will do their best to get it for you, they also have a free trial period, they let you get your feet wet with their product directory and supplier. This is great because you can see if they have your niche product available for dropshipping before you pay a membership fee, you won't be able to view the suppliers contact information or place an order, but you will be able to get a good idea how they operate and if they have enough inventory for your particular niche, salehoo price starts at about $67 a year, it gives you access to the directory of suppliers, training material and members forum, they also have ready to go websites that have built in search engine optimization. They have a large design from a variety of templates

## Drop ship access

www.dropshipaccess.com on this site you can gain access to dropshipping for free for seven days so that you can view all the products that are available, they have everything from books, music, electronics, jewelry, lingerie, and software. You get access to over two million different products at wholesale price, the free trial will not give you the prices of the products but the prices ranges from 30 to 70 percent of mark (manufacturer's suggested retail price).

After the free trial period, you will be charged $49.95 per month; you will have to give your credit card information when you sign up for the free trial. If you do not wish to continue make sure you delete your membership information before the free trial period expires, they also have a system set up with a push to market service for eBay, it will easily post products for sale on eBay. If items are running low they will send you an email to notify you. Dropship access offers automatic updates, this mean that if a product is out of stock it will automatically update your website.

## Dropship design

www.dropshipdesign.com this site also dropship to other countries other than the U.S. But, you will need to contact them in advance. Dropship design is one of the easiest ways to get into the dropshipping business, they have readymade websites and is eBay certified, which make it easy to list products on eBay, they have several plans to meet the seller's needs from amateur dropshipping to the most experienced dropshipper. They have a return policy so you won't have to worry about returns because they handle the whole process for you, they also have automatic updates relating to inventory and prices of products, you will be notified when products are getting low or out of stock and when the product is being shipped you will receive a tracking number that you can give to your customer dropshippers

## Dropshippers

www.dropshippers.com this site is not recommended for beginners, but if you are a quick learner, you'll be ok or you can just switch to it after you have gotten the hang of dropshipping, they offer some advance tools and is one of the best dropshippers out there. Dropshipper offers access to more than 3.5 million products they have the largest directory in the U.S.

You can gain access to their whole directory for a one-time fee of $99 . You'll have access to wholesaler's dropshippers and discount closeout and surplus item with their website plan, they still give you a website pre-loaded with products that are picked by you and the design of your website can be customized by you through the installed control panel. They will even set up a merchant account for you, they also have a free trial period of seven days so that you can check the service out before you commit to a setup fee.

## Wholesale2b

www.wholesale2b.com with this website you can get your dropshipping business set and running quickly, they have about 1.5 million products and have a great customer service, they also have readymade websites and is eBay certified, you'll get access to 250 different auction templates, there is not a limit on how many products that you can list on eBay for auction, they have several plans to choose from, starting price at $24.99 a month on the faq page they have answers to most of the basic questions. You can also sign up for a free trial where you can view the product and their price list, if you decide to go with wholesale2b you can purchase one of the three plans that they have.

## Sunrise wholesale merchandise

www.sunrisewholesalemerchandise.com this dropshipping site specialize in home and beauty products, furniture, and toys. They only have a little over 10,000 products, they do have tools for instant access to dropshipping products with online ordering and they have a day return policy. This dropshipper will help you build a website to sell your products, they have plenty of templates that you can choose from, and you can add and remove products and change categories.

## Product sourcing

www.productsourcing.com this site has a nice selection of products to choose from, they also allow free access to viewing their drop shipping products but offer limited access, you won't be able to use any of their tools and tutorials, they won't be available unless you purchase their premium account, they have no return policy or warranty, if your customer receives damaged or lost merchandise they are not responsible, they do offer tracking when the product is shipped, there is no readymade website or any automatic update tools that will keep you informed of any changes. So it would be your responsibility to keep up with the latest information. Here are some more drop shipping services that you can check out:

www.aidandtrade.com
www.electronixhq.com
www.focalprice.com
www.hienotedirectory.com
www.nationaldropshippers.com
www.plumislandsilver.com
www.truedropshippers.com
www.urbanload.com
www.wholesalecentral.com

## Processing payments

The online payment process can be a bit confusing at first glance, but once you have used it a few time you'll get used to it fast, some shopping carts offer multiple plans to accommodate your preferred method of processing payments, some shopping carts have a merchant account and a payment gateway, you will need real time credit card processing so that when your customer inputs their credit card information into your payment processor, within a few seconds, the money will be taken off the customer's credit card and is on its way to your bank account then the customer will receive an order confirmation. You have several options that you can choose for payments, and that is a merchant account or PayPal, which will allow you to receive payment from anyone that has a PayPal account themselves, a merchant account will allow you to process payments credit cards. Merchant accounts and PayPal accounts has certain restrictions and has fees with every transaction. A merchant account is basically an agreement with a bank to let you accept credit cards. A payment gateway is a service that authorizes and process the payment securely. Here are two websites that you can use as a merchant account to process orders: www.streamline.com and www.1shoppingcart.com and you can use www.worldpay.com as your payment gateway provider. 1shoppingcart has affiliate programs built in getting a merchant account when you're just starting out, it is not easy, it requires good credit, and if your credit is not up to par then you will have to use a high risk merchant account. It charges a bit more every month and you will also have to pay a higher percentage on every sale you make for a shopping cart system, you will need to be able to connect your shopping cart to your bank. In order to do this, you will need a payment gateway, your payment gateway works as a guarantee that the credit card transaction goes through without any problems. Credit card companies like MasterCard and VISA won't process any money without a payment gateway to protect itself against fraud or misuse of credit card information, the payment gateway basically protects you and your customer from credit card scams which sometimes doesn't work but it does help. The payment gateway will confirm that there is enough funds in the account and then charges the account. The payment gateway is where the money gets collected and transported back and forth, from one account to another. It serves as an intermediary for your merchant account to your payment platform.

For your website, you can create this yourself but since you're just starting you may want to pay someone to do this for you, your payment platform, this could be your PayPal or your shopping cart like, www.ultracart.com. It will require additional items, a gateway processor and merchant account that you could set up through a bank, a great gateway service company like www.authorize.net this site will allow you to create links for your products connected to your payment gateway, and notifies your dropshipper that they need to send the product to your customer, it's best to find a merchant account first because there are plenty of gateway companies to choose from, once you have found a merchant account they will give you a code and will transfer your money to your account after each sale.

# Gateway Processes

Here are some more gateway processors that will give you codes that you will have to link to your order buttons.
www.1shoppingcart.com
www.2checkout.com
www.googlecheckout.com
www.paypal.com
www.sagepay.com
www.worldpay.com

## PayPal

PayPal is one of the most popular payment systems we have today, even though everyone don't have a PayPal account. Most online shoppers shop more on online stores that accepts PayPal payment, but in order to accept PayPal payments, the customer must have a PayPal account. PayPal is free to set up and the customer is charged nothing when they purchase a product, however when payments comes in, you are charged a fee, the downside is that the money is not paid into your bank account, it goes into your virtual PayPal account. When you want the money you have in your Paypal account in your local bank account, you log in into your Paypal account and transfer the money into your bank account. PayPal deducts its commission as soon as they receive it.

## Google wallet

Google wallet is like PayPal and does not cost anything upfront, the fees are almost the same as PayPal but with a per transaction fee, they also take a percentage of the transaction, the fees are based on your monthly sales volume. To be able to get a Google wallet you would have to sign up here:
http://www.wallet.google.com they will ask you for personal contact information plus information related to your business when you sign up, you will have to integrate Google Wallet with your dropshipping website.

## 2checkout

www.2checkout.com if you are selling internationally or domestically then this site is your best option they accept a variety of payments methods. With 2checkout you will get paid weekly and there is no set up fees, gateway, monthly, recurring billing, the best thing about 2checkout is that they give you a free trial before you get committed. You can sign up using this link https://www.2checkout.com/signup

Here are some website that you can check out.
www.stripe.com
www.payments.amazon.com allows only amazon customers to pay on your website without entering their credit card information.
www.clickbank.com
www.gocardless.com
www.e-junkie.com
www.rapbank.com

Websites to design your shop:
www.ultracart.com
www.actinic.com
www.agoracart.com
www.1and1.com
www.bigcommerce.com
www.cubecart.com
www.3dcart.com
www.pinnaclecart.com
www.webstore.amazon.com

# Hosting companies

Here are some hosting companies to help you get started with your website; these are some of the top companies out there, most review sites stand by these companies and the services they provide to their customers.

## Godaddy
www.godaddy.com This hosting company, if you are planning on using Wordpress based website, they offer email forwarding, photo galleries, blogging, and preinstalled software apps starting at $9.99 per month.

## Landl
www.landl.com is a well-established hosting company; they offer several different hosting packages starting at $4.99. The smaller packages have restrictions on server space, email accounts, and sql database, but for $9.99 you can get unlimited of everything, when you choose the second or third level package you'll get a free domain name plus unlimited web space. 1and1 offer a wide selection of services, products, tools and features and customer support as well as a professional website builder.

## Hostgator
www.hostgator.com is one of the top hosting companies out there today, they offer 24/7 tech support, and they offer unlimited email address, bandwidth and disk space with free shopping cart software, message forums, membership scripts, photo galleries, site building tools and many of website templates, they also have unlimited domain for a little bit more money prices at $10.99 a month. Photograph of yourself on your site, by having a photograph on your site will let people know who they are dealing with and that you are a real person. If you don't like your own photograph then you can create an avatar with these website s listed below:
www.cartoonyourworld.com, www.mywebface.com
www.sitepal.com a site that provides security image to make your site trustworthy. You can have a great looking website, but if

you don't have security measures that customers are looking for in order to hand over their credit card information, you can lose a sale. Security icons: this is one of the quickest and easiest way to let your customer know that your website is safe to shop at. Companies like TRUST will review your website and they have security standards that they follow, if your site meets their standards they will give you permission to hold their icon on your website.

## Disclaimer

If you have a site that has anything to do with wealth building or health or even have information and products that could be harmful, then you can download these free legal policies for your website from www.seqlegal.com or you can just search for one in Google.

## Sitemap

You should have a sitemap on your website if you want Google to find all the information on your site; you can install the xml sitemap plugin here at this website. http://wordpress.org/extend/plugins/xml-sitemap. Feed and it will be done for you.

## Copyright policy

At the bottom of every page of your website, you should have a copyright 2019 all rights reserved. This is to protect your intellectual property from people who may try to steal your content testimonials. It's important to have visible testimonials that will help persuade people to purchase your product or services. In About Us page, you should put a photograph of yourself or an avatar on the about us page. People will want to know who they are buying from, it creates credibility for your site and you increase your chances of people buying from you . It builds trust, some people will make a buying decision based on what they read on your about us page, so it's very important to have an about us page on your site.

# Home page

Your home page must tell people what they are expected to find and what it's all about. This is very important because if you don't, they will leave your site more quickly. Google analytics is a great tool to use for your website. It tells you the number of daily, weekly, and monthly visitors you have. It also tells you your sites page views, bounce rate; this is when a visitor leaves your site without looking at another page, they also tell you from which search engine your visitor came from, traffic source , how visitors found your site and how long they stayed. This is one of the most important features this has too, it tells you which keywords were used to find your website. It's important to have Google analytic on each page of your website that sells a product or service, so you can see which one of your pages that no one ever looks at, you should put Google analytic on all of your websites and you only have to sign up once, once you sign up, Google will give you a code that you put on your website, they have a tutorial that will walk you through the whole process: www.google.com/analytics and it's free.

Here are some more analytics tools that you can use:
www.accesswatch.com
www.extremtracking.com
www.statecounter.com
All of these sites are free.

## Valuable content

You must provide your customers with valuable content and product reviews newsletters, blog post, articles and tip of the day/week/month and so on. The thing about content is that it must be informative, while not being promotional, sales pitches is not considered being valuable content. People questions are also a good form of content, here are some questions and answers websites where you can find peoples questions and answers in your niche www.answers.com and www.theanswerbank.com. Google keyword planner, you can use keyword planner to find keywords for your niche to get traffic to your website. In order to use Google keyword planner you would have to sign up for Google rewards account.

There a number of other tools available.

 www.goodkeywords.com
 www.keywordspy.com
 www.keyworddiscovery.com
 www.keywordelite.com
 www.longtailpro.com
 www.ppcwebspy.com
 www.senuke.com
 www.wordtracker.com
 www.webmaster-toolkit.com

You must publish your website, submit your site to Google here http://www.google.com/submit_content.html or you can just Google "add url", you must submit your website so that Google will see it quicker, submit your site to demos here: http://www.dmoz.org/add.html. Demos has a large database of human added websites by having a backlink from them to your site will increase the amount of traffic you receive if you don't get listed here on your first attempt for some reason, just make some changes to your website and try again. Submit your website to Bing. http://www.bing.com/toolbox/submit-site-uri. Submit your site to yahoo http://search.yahoo.com/info/submit.html. After you have summited your site to search engines, you can check if Google has found it by going to www.yourwebsitehere.com. Here Google will show you your site and show the pages it has indexed, if a Google message displays shows up, "your site did not match any documents", It means that Google have not indexed your site yet, you can also try typing your url into the search box at www.google.com if your site appears in the results, that means that Google has indexed it, if your site is not indexed just submit it again, you could also use www.addme.com to manual submit your site to 14 search engines.

Learn from your competitors, you would want to find out how your competitors got to the first page of Google, this is where you want your site to be. There a couple of ways to do this, you can learn from your competitors, you must always keep an eye on your competitors in any business you're in. The first thing you must do is find out what keywords they rank for to get on the first page. You can search for keywords in your niche to see what domain name pops up click on each domain name on the website, then put your cursor over the page and right click then choose the "view source" this should give you the source code of the web pages.

Screenshot of source code page, here you would be able to see the page the way Google sees it. View the source code of the first five to ten domain names, you should do a screenshot of the web site to see what keywords they are suing to get on the first page of Google.

You can find out how your competitors sites are optimized by using www.webceo.com and www.spufu.com for a fee after doing your research you need to develop your site so that you can outrank your competitors and so that Google will see your site as more relevant, there is not really a rule here it's mostly trial and error.

You just have to do your research and learn things you need to do to beat the competitors, make sure your site is easy to navigate, offer relevant content and valuable information relating to your product, make sure your products description are detailed with quality images, have keywords to describe your service or product. The quality of your site will have a big impact on the business you receive so add value to your product with relevant information related to the product.

# Page Rank

As you are becoming more familiar with SEO tactics, you will learn what PageRank is. PageRank is a scale between 0 to 10. 10 being the highest rank that you can get on Google, this is how Google ranks the relevance of the content on your site, pertaining to a particular niche product or service the higher the page rank the better the chances are that your website will be one of the first to be seen when someone Google's your niche with your keywords. You can use Firefox on this site www.mozilla.org to measure Google page rank for your site when you use Firefox as your browser, the page rank for your site will be shown, your site will start with a PageRank of 0, and it will be harder to appear on the first page of Google if you have other sites in your niche with a higher page rank of over 4.
 You'll find that it will be hard to beat them but it can be done with good SEO tactics. Let me give you an example how PageRank really works, let's say you have a website on pit bulls, but it's not getting any visitors because you're not on the first page of Google for any of the keywords that you use so Google thinks that your site is not important because you're not getting any traffic so Google gives your site a low PageRank which starts at zero, which means you have no backlinks at all ( i will explain backlinks in the next chapter).
PageRank is mostly based on relevant quality content and backlinks.

Some people might find your site and link to it from theirs, when people link to your website your page rank goes up to pri, now a high authority website on breeding pit bull with a page rank 9 links to your website.

That will make your page rank go up because Google can see that someone important has link to your site. If you can get high authority websites in your niche to link to your website, your page rank will most likely rise.
Google like to see websites links to other relevant sites the more relevant links that you have, the better your chances are of getting a higher page rank.

**Backlink**

A backlink is basically linking from one website to another, when Google looks at backlinks to a site it checks the page rank of the site the link is coming from. A backlink from a website with a page rank of 8 will be of great use rather than having one with a pri anchor text of a backlink, it's important that you understand the concept of anchor text because it's how Google decides the relevance of your site. So, how to get these backlinks by contacting websites in your niche with high page ranks and asking them to put a link on their site to yours. If someone mentions your website with a hyperlink in social media, like Facebook, Google can see that and it may help your site obtain a higher Page rank.

# Getting traffic to your website

There are literally hundreds of ways to get traffic to your website, if you are lucky enough to rank on the first page of Google you're pretty much good to go but if not, always try to improve your SEO. If you are not ranking high in Google, so let us start with some shopping directories, a shopping directory is a website that has a list of other websites and they categorize them in a certain order pertaining to niches. You can look at the websites that are in your niche that might be of interest to you, then sign up and submit your site to the directories, these are a great resource for getting backlinks.

Here are a list of directories that you can check out:

www.megashpbot.com

www.pricegrabber.com

www.shopzilla.com

www.shopping.com

www.google.com/merchants, on this site you can list your product in the Shopping results in Google.

Press release, when you post a press release about your new product or service, other sites will automatically post it on their website this is a great way to get extra traffic to your site; you can use press release to promote the launch of your new website or to just let people know what you are offering, you can also optimize your press release for keywords that you are targeting. It will help you rank in Google, you can outsource the writing of your press release here: www.writinghelptools.com and www.elance.com a lot of press release sites are free and some you have to pay for, but they usually guarantee that yours will be picked up by a major search engine.

Here are some press release sites that are free.

www.businesswire.com

www.free-press-release.com

www.i-newswire.com

www.prweb.com

www.prlog.com

www.webwire.com

You can find more press release sites just by 'Googling' "press release submission service".

# Video marketing

Video marketing is one of the best ways to market a product or service. Google loves videos; they can help your page rank for your website too.

You can submit videos with links to your website, to the list of websites below most of the website are free but some you might have to open an account, make sure that you use keywords in your title and description when you submit your video.

Here are some video sites you can use:
www.youtube.com
http://video.google.com
www.vimeo.com
www.buzznet.com
www.dailymotion.com
www.flixya.com
www.gofish.com
www.metacafe.com
www.instant-traffic-geyser.com
www.screenjunkies.com
www.tubetoolbox.com
www.video.yahoo.com
www.tubemogul.com

On this site, you can have your video uploaded automatically up to 20 video hosting sites at www.viralvideochart.com. You can find the most popular viral videos. Pay-Per-Click ( PPC), this is where you would have to bid on keywords in your niche, this is one of the best ways to get traffic to your website, and you only have to pay when a person clicks on your ad. Thousands, when launching an ad campaign could see your ad, when a user types in your keywords into the search engine: the advertising network will show your ad, so the traffic that you will receive will be niche targeted, the only thing you have to do to get started is to decide what keywords you want to pay for when someone clicks on your ad. You will also have to decide how much you want to pay per click; you can set a daily budget and can stop your ads from showing at any time if you are not making any money on the ad. You can also track how much your ads are costing and track how many people have visited your site through the ad.

**Paid traffic:** Below are some more pay-per-click network sites that you can research, they will post your ad on websites and search engines.

www.7search.com they advertise on the smaller search engines. They are cheapest and high converting. www.cliksor.com

www.clickbooth.com
www.clicksor.com
www.chitika.com
http://adwords.google.com

This site will get you a lot of traffic; the downside is that the cost per click is much higher than other pay per click networks.

www.advertising.microsoft.com/home
www.adbull.com
www.adcenter.microsoft.com
www.advertise.com
www.bing.com
www.burstmedia.com
www.doubleclick.com
www.marchex.com
www.findology.com
www.leadimpact.com

If you want to use more than one pay-per-click network you can use: www.prosper202.com to manage them all and compare their performances.

## Traffic with eBay

www.ebay.com you can go to the classified section on eBay and post an ad for about $10 for 30 days, you can place the ad in your niche category.

## Traffic with reviews

www.reveiwme.com you can get traffic to your site here, bloggers get paid to do reviews and promote other people's products.

## Traffic with amazon

www.amazon.com amazon is not only for shopping, you can also advertise on here to get traffic to your site, if you would look under the product on amazon you will find sponsored links, this is where your advertisement would go.

## Traffic with Facebook ads

www.facebook.com/ads, here you can place an ad in your chosen niche category.

You can also sign up with some mobile phone networks to advertise, here are some companies that advertise on mobile phones, they charge per click.

www.adsmobi.com
www.google.com/ads/admob
www.inmobi.com
www.invoca.com
www.mojiva.com

## Traffic with top link

www.toplink.com helps you build valuable networks on the top networking sites, each social networking site has its own (invite me list), there are invite me list for:

- Facebook
- LinkedIn
- Twitter
- Myspace
- Xing
- Bebo
- Academy

- Friendster
- Hi5
- Connects
- Blue chip expert
- affluence .org
- Naymz
- Orkut
- Perfect network
- Plaxo
- Tagged
- Unky
- Viadeo

## Traffic with Clickbank

www.clickbank.com/advertise this site offers advertising for vendors who want visibility for their product or service, your ads can be placed in any marketplace category, if you have a digital product, like an eBook or any other digital product then you can sign up with clickbank, and affiliates will sell your product for you. Other ways to make money, no website needed, use Facebook and Twitter to make money. You sign up on Facebook and Twitter then find people in your niche and just follow and add people as friends and then you can start promoting your products or you can find a digital product on clickbank and send it to them.

Make money from blogs, you can find a blog in your niche and ask the blogger if they would like to do a joint venture were you can promote a digital product to their blog and split the profits, make money from how you can write an article for eHow and then put your affiliate link at the bottom. Google loves eHow, just type in "how to" or "how to make" and that article will show up on the first page of Google.

Make money from blogging, www.payperpost.com on this you can be paid for blogging.

Make money from freelance work, you can make a good living doing freelance work if you have some kind of special skill, this is basically outsourcing, where people hire you to do a task that they don't have time to do or don't know how to do, below are some websites to check out:

www.99centarticle.com
www.agentsofvalue.com
www.elance.com
www.fiverr.com
www.freelancer.com
www.microworkers.com
www.mturk.com
www.need-an-article.net
www.odeskresources.com
www.peopleperhour.com

Make money to socialize, there are companies out there that will pay you just to talk about their products online using social media. Make money on websites by reading email;

Here are a list of sites you can check out.

www.automatedsocialmedia.com
www.cashunite.com
www.chatabout.com
www.loop88.com
www.mylikes.com
www.paidsocialmediajobs.com
www.postloop.com

Make money with your art, there are plenty of sites out there that are looking for freelance artists, check these sites out:

www.artfire.com
www.artdeadlinelist.com
www.avatarpress.com
www.cape-shore.com
www.crowdspring.com
www.exceltree.com
www.funnytimes.com
www.leanintree.com
www.zazzle.com
http://www.oatmealstudios.com

Make money with your smartphone, here are some websites that will pay you to do jobs like taking a "selfie" holding a product. Visit these sites for information:

www.checkpoint.com
www.gigwalk.com

www.junowallet.com
www.staree.com

Make money creating and selling music, there are a lot of music making software programs that you can use to make music, iTunes is one of the best places to sell your music online, and you can tinker with these programs until you learn the ropes, once you have several tracks, you can upload them to these sites to sell. You can sell your music on these sites:

www.bandcamp.com
www.cdbaby.com
www.dittomusic.com
www.itunes.com
www.musicmagpie.co.uk
www.songstall.com
www.soundcloud.com
www.tunecore.com

Make money selling arts and craft products, you can make money selling your arts and crafts on these sites:

www.artfire.com
www.artpal.com
www.ebay.com
www.etsy.com
www.folksy.com
www.zazzle.com

Make money being a "how to" writer. Many people love to read "how-to-books".

Here are some websites that are looking for freelance writers to write for them.

www.allbusiness.com
www.allexperts.com
www.answerbag.com
www.answer.com
www.answers.yahoo.com
www.ask.com
www.blurtit.com
www.businesssinsider.com
www.chacha.com
www.chegg.com
www.createpool.com
www.doityourself.com
www.ehow.com
www.factmonster.com
www.financialhighway.com
www.fluther.com
www.howstuffworks.com
www.inewidea.com
www.justanswers.com
www.knowbrainers.com
www.makeuseof.com
www.soyouwanna.com
www.stackexchange.com
www.theanswerbank.com
www.webanswers.com
www.wikianswer.com

Make money on websites by reading emails;
You can make money reading emails and responding to them, check these websites out:

www.inboxdollars.com
www.donkeymails.com

Make money playing games, there are a number of websites that will pay you to play video games check these out:

www.game-tester.net
www.gamesville.com
www.gamesreadar.com

Make money reading emails, there are some companies out there that are willing to pay you to find out what people are saying about their products, services, websites such as www.hotmail.com , this is an email marketing company with customer feedback

Make money watching advert, www.youdata.com believes that promoting a product will be more successful when the marketing is targeted at a certain niche.

Here is how to get started:

Register and create a "me file"

You have to answer some questions about yourself, this will determine the type of commercials you will receive.

The advertisements that fit your profile will be sent to you alone with the amount that the advertiser will pay.

Your data gives you payments for watching commercials and will also give incentives to those who get more people to sign up, they pay you via PayPal.

# Make money from fiverr

www.fiverr.com is a site where you can get almost every service that you think of, if you think you have a talent of some sort, you could offer your services for $5, this is a site where you can start making money very quickly and there are no membership fees and no bidding. it's easy to use and free to sign up to get started, all you have to do is, register to get an account and start posting your offers, it's best to browse the site to see what's in demand then make your offer a little better.

I know that $5 may not seem like a lot of money, but if you can automate your service or place multiple listings, you can earn decent money from this site, this site gets millions of visitors a month, sellers are ranked by levels and are able to achieve a higher seller level by getting your offer featured based on a variety of factors by getting a volume of your services delivered satisfactorily you could increase your level of positive feedback and reviews from buyers will help your levels rise, when you achieve top seller status, you can offer prices more than $5. All services starts at $5, which are called gigs , but as a top seller you can offer an up sale of your service, you could also make money off fiverr by reselling their cheap service on other freelance sites like odesk or elance.

Here is a list of freelance sites that you can earn money with:

www.agentsofvalue.com
www.guru.com
www.clickchores.com
www.ifreelance.com
www.domystuff.com
www.microworkers.com
www.fieldagents.com
www.mturk.com
www.freelance.com
www.odesk.com

Sell gift cards at www.giftcardgranny.com you can make money with unwanted gift cards.

Find discounted products and freebies and sell them. There are many websites that gives away free stuff or sell merchandise at a discounted price, you can get the m and then sell them, check these websites out to find products:

www.groupola.com
www.groupon.com
www.gumtree.com
www.mightydeal.com
www.wowcher.com

Create a marketing profile, build a marketing profile by telling a genuine authentic story distributed through strong marketing challenges, while also improving sales, you would want to have a presence on social media to get your name out there.

You will need to develop a communication strategy, which takes in-dept planning, and research with social media, this can be done easily, and you will need to focus on your audiences, messaging and goals.

Your audiences should be the most important aspect of your com munication strategy, you would need to answer some key questions to turn your audience into prospects, who are these people, and where did they come from? Knowing that you have an audience what are you going to say? How are you going to keep their attention? This is when you make your elevator pitch, what makes your product or service a good fit for this audience? What problems are you solving that your competitors are not solving? This could be a unique product, pricing, or service.

Create strategies to communicate your service or product to your audience with keyword messaging, like:

- Email marketing
- A blog that promotes your message in an informative way.
- Adwords
- Direct mail
- Newsletter
- Articles in industry newsletters
- Goals

Your goals should point to sales growth, if your business is unknown, you would need to use communication to build a reputation because if you are unknown in your market you will need to inform and educate your existing audience with valuable content by flooding the market with your message.

Once you have your message and tactics down pack, set realistic goals, look for ways to get your message to your prospects, such as with blog posts, social media, mailing list, compare this with other traffic to determine overall effectiveness, storytelling. Every great book and marketing campaign has one thing in common and that is a great story in internet marketing, you have to focus your energy on getting your message across in a way that captures your audience attention with banner ads, posts, tweets, etc. It's ok to be brief in your marketing, but don't let your story suffer from just telling stories, set your message apart from others and help your point to become clear.

The internet is the world's biggest marketing platform, it influences how people communicate, by engaging your prospects with valuable interesting information; you will keep their attention and will turn these prospects into customers, by creating your own marketing content and distribution system through Email blast, Twitter, and Facebook followers. You'll start to get some traction and reach your goal by educating, informing and persuading people to buy your products or services.

If you have ever posted anything on Facebook, Twitter, or Instagram, then you already have experience in the social sharing ecosystem that has taken over traditional channels to distribute information. By building a reliable communication channel with your prospects it will pay off down the road, because you would have built trust and it will show you as an up-and-coming, and as a leader in your niche product or service.

# Ebook writing

An eBook in your niche will offer a lot of marketing opportunities, it adds credibility to your niche product or service, and it increases your chances. To be a publishing source, writing your own eBook has never been easier, even though there are millions of eBook on the market, you can still gain a share or even dominate your niche market, by writing an eBook, you can exclude your competitors and it will add credibility to your brand, it offers a way to be viewed as an expert in your niche, your eBook can educate prospects and help you ace your product or service. You will hear me mention eBook a lot, let me explain why. eBook is an electronic product and it's easy to create, when creating an eBook in your niche, you create multiple streams of income; every new product is a new stream of income. An eBook have a 100% profit margin because it's a digital product, it doesn't matter if you sell one or a thousand, the cost is still the same; zero, it provides instant gratification because once the customer purchase it they can download it, they can download it to electronic device, computer, laptop, phones, etc. You add value to people lives by giving them valuable information and a solution to their problems, you can enlist hundreds of affiliates to sell your eBook and they will sell it to people around the world. When creating your eBook you need to put it into PDF format, make sure to embed all fonts so that everyone who purchased the eBook will be able to use it on their device; mac users can read it also.

The following websites will convert your eBook into pdf format for you:

www.acrobat.com
www.nuance.com/pdfconverter
www.fineprint.com

You can also use these websites to design the cover of your eBook:

www.absolutecovers.com
www.coverfactory.com
www.ebookcovercreator.com
www.ecoverexpert.com

If you don't have the time to write an eBook in your niche, you could outsource to have your eBook written for you on these sites:

www.elance.com

www.freelancer.com

www.guru.com

Creating an eBook is what gives you leverage, for example, by having affiliates, blogs, mailing list, joint venture, and your website, all selling your eBook for you. You could dominate your niche, you could pay $50 to join www.clickbank.com as a vendor, you will then be able to sell your eBook and have affiliates sell it for you through their marketplace after you have created your eBook, and you will also need to create a website. Try www.homewebsitecenter.com, here you can create your website in three easy steps, then fill in your PayPal address and your website is ready, you could even add upgrades, if you want the free version your website will be ready in ten minutes, when building your website, you will only need two pages; a sales page where people can find out more about your product

and buy it and a thank you page where customers can download you product.

# Building a mailing list

I have talked about mailing list in the earlier chapters of this book, so now I'm going to talk about building your mailing list to make it plain and simple, you build your mailing list simply by driving traffic to your opt-in page, the more traffic you get to your opt-in page the faster you grow your mailing list.

I'm going to explain why it's so important to build your mailing list, let me give you an example; let's say you have 10,000 subscribers to your opt-in list that want to receive information from you on a regular basis by giving the people that opt-in to your mailing list valuable content, you have to built trust with them. When you have created an eBook in that niche with more informative information those 10,000 subscribers will be more inclined to purchase your product because you have built that trust with them. Just think that you have 10,000 prospects at your fingertips, whenever you have a product or service to sell. That's money on demand! Not only can you sell your own product to them, you could also sell them other people's product from affiliate sites like clickbank .com, your profit potential could be endless after you get the swing of things, you could find a new niche and repeat the whole process. This is called multiple streams of income.

By having a mailing list of subscribers, means that you control the traffic to your website for free just by sending out an email to your opt-in list, more traffic equals free money. Basically, what I'm saying is that you could build a mailing list once and make money forever, all you have to do is drive traffic to your opt-in-page so that your prospects can get added to your mailing list, then you can direct them to any website or blog you want for years.

Now let's get into how to build your mailing list, since you understand its value, after you have chosen your target market for example, dating advice, health care, and making money online, now you can start the design of your opt-in-page.

I recommend visiting several internet marketer's opt-in-page to see what it looks like and model the design. You can copy the precise formula they use to capture targeted subscribers. You will also need to get an autoresponder service provider you can try:

www.getresponse.com it allows you to automatically send out a series of e-mails to your subscribers whenever you want. You could also hire a web designer from elance .com or vworkers .com to set up your autoresponder to your website. Driving traffic to your opt-in-page, there are plenty of ways to drive traffic to your opt-in-page by using:

- facebook
- fiverr
- twitter
- youtube
- clickbank affiliates
- facebook groups
- facebook profile
- pay-per-click
- SEO
- cost-per-action leads
- solo ads
- banner advertising and so on.

I am going into detail on how to use some of these sites to grow your mailing list by the thousands, it's not that hard, you just have to be willing to spend the money to get there.

I'm going to share with you a few strategies to build your mailing list.

You could buy gigs on fiverr.com. It's possible to grow your list by the thousands, by buying gigs on this website, a gig is when you have someone on fiverr.com to promote your offers to their mailing list, Facebook page , twitter followers, etc. for five dollars. If you buy a hundred gigs on fiverr to promote you free offers, it would cost you just $500. Fiverr.com is a website where people are willing to do things for

$5. You're able to post things you need done or you can post a service that you want to perform.

You could use pay-per-click advertising via Google adwords, yahoo or any other pay-per-click advertising services. Pay-per-click is when a website owner pays an advertiser such as Google every time someone clicks their ad. Every time a certain word is typed into a search engine it will trigger your ad to appear as a sponsored link.

You can advertise on Google content network by setting up an account at www.google.com/adword/displaynetwork and you will be able to get banner ads created for you for just $20 at: www.20dollarbanners.com

You could also do solo ads. A solo ad is where you pay someone to send out emails to their mailing list for you, you could use solo ad provider like:webstars2k:  http://webstar2k.com/ezines

Try doing ad swaps, it's best to do this after you have a large number of people already on your mailing list. It is a great list building tool to use without spending a dime. All you have to do is a couple of joint ventures or ad swaps every month, just email your list for them and they would email their list for you, driving traffic to each other's opt-in-pages by doing ad swaps you can grow your list fast.

Check out these sites: www.imadswaps.com, http://adswapfinder.com, and http://safe-swaps.com. Here is another website where you can rent more than 50,000 mailing list in different niches http://list.nextmark.com you must always be aware of the spam rule, when doing mailing list as swaps using other peoples mailing list to make sure your website don't get blocked for spam. It's best to have a blog that you can send traffic to with links back to your website, this is important so that your efforts to drive traffic to your sites opt-in-page won't get tagged as spam. Search engine optimization (SEO) is the process for improving your website's visibility with natural search results, using keywords, SEO looks for what keywords people are searching for to improve the rank of a website. The higher your websites rank in the search results, the better the chances of people seeing it. If you are able to get your website on the first page of Google by using keywords, means that a lot of free traffic and free traffic means free money.

For example, let's say that there are over 5,000,000 searches a month for the key word "football", if your football related website is listed on the first page of results whenever someone type in the word "football" in the search results of Google, then you can expect to get tens of thousands of visitors to your site each month when it comes on with SEO, every keyword typed into the search engine is a market to target and profit from. Some strategies involves using long tail keywords. For example; keywords like "washington D.C. one-bedroom apartment" rather than just "apartment" by going after long tail keywords you will have a better chance because the competition is low you can use this suggestion when you build your website. Google uses hundreds of different indicators in it's algorithm to determine how relevant your website is to a specific search query, these indicators also include relevant content on your site and the number of sites linking back to your website, how long your website has been up, and how often your site is updated etc. What matters the most is the content you have on your site, it should be relevant to the keyword, and backlinks linking to your site, some recommended tools for getting links to your site.

www.bruteforcesec.com a great link building tool at $150 per month.

www.buildmyrank.com starts at $59 per month. At www.fiverr.com you can buy backlinks. www.onlywire.com lets you auto submit your online content to the top social media sites with one click.

http://massarticlesubmitter.net.

www.serpassist.com a great automated tool, $97 per month.

# COMING SOON!!!!!

SELF MADE MILLIONAIRE

MONEY MADE SIMPLE

THE SELF EXPLAINED GUIDE
TO ONLINE IDENTITY